WALKING BACKWARDS

WALKING BACKWARDS

LEE SHARKEY

TUPELO PRESS
North Adams, Massachusetts

Library of Congress Cataloging-in-Publication Data available upon request.

ISBN: 978-1-936797-90-5

Cover and text designed by Howard Klein.

Cover painting: Anonymous, twentieth century. "Pogroms," circa 1915 (Jewish refugees after a pogrom in Russia). Oil on cardboard, 71.5 x 57 cm. Judaica Collection Max Berger. Photo credit: Erich Lessing /Art Resource. Used with permission.

First paperback edition: October 2016.

Tupelo Press

P.O. Box 1767, North Adams, Massachusetts 01247

Telephone: (413) 664-9611 /editor@tupelopress.org /www.tupelopress.org

Tupelo Press is an award-winning independent literary press that publishes fine fiction, nonfiction, and poetry in books that are a joy to hold as well as read. Tupelo Press is a registered 501(c)(3) nonprofit organization, and we rely on public support to carry out our mission of publishing extraordinary work that may be outside the realm of the large commercial publishers. Financial donations are welcome and are tax deductible.

In memory of Abraham Sutzkever and Peretz Markish,
whom neither Hitler nor Stalin could silence

For Martha, sister in poetry

CONTENTS

CAUTIONARIES

I

Pry an old woman loose from her house—
she and her legs refuse to leave,
she and her mouth refuse to eat.
Therefore, she is different from paper.

She can set up camp before the door,
she can shake her shoes till the clods fall off,
she can be a ladder climbed by thought
as her bones rock back and forth.

2

After the old man died by fire he thought he had done enough.
He settled down in a village of stone and befriended his orchard.
He invited the children to gather apricots.
He invited the students to room in his house of stone;
they were serious and polite.

The council said, *They are not for us.*
The neighbors said, *You are not* of *us.*
The old man, smelling fire, was surprised, but not so surprised.

3

In the morning a mother turned toward her son.
The wind was sifting his hair and riffling his t-shirt.
She uncovered the half of his face that had not been ruined
for the light to shine on—
a kindness to him and to herself.
Now he owns nothing and rests in the place
where the one who laughs maniacally
cannot find him to be quieted by him.

4

It was enough that we killed the brother
but when sometime later we returned for the sister
shame went looking for a place to lay its head.
The barracks were occupied, the palace shuttered.

Shame took up its wanderings, everywhere
pressing its face to windows, calling
At long last, here is your shame
and we thought we heard something uncoiling deep in the shells of our ears.

5

After 400 years in a tin coffin
Tycho's spine is the color of mahogany.
It rests like a seahorse on the floor of the operating theater,
it flexes like a maiden's braid.

Inside, on the helical staircase,
spirits ascend/descend by mercury lantern.
You who are seeking the secret of death here,
there is no death here.

6

I slipped into the skirts of Rosa Luxemburg
and crossed the border to foment the revolution.
I was felled by fever.
I typeset *What Next?* in secret
with a crew of fly-by-night compositors.
Every night we commandeered a print shop;
presses clattered out the great new day.

$\qquad\qquad\qquad\qquad$ Even now,

a century later: ink stain on my fingers.

7

Because the hands remembered what they had done
they exiled themselves from the house of the body.
From time to time they crept to the back door
where the kitchen girl would toss them scraps

and the hands, a little bit in love,
would do errands for her—tie her laces,
shelter the flame for her cigarette—
while her face drifted off to the war.

8

Any sound that a sound might make has lost its history.
Look no further than the country of limestone and fir
whose lost name whips in the wind like an anthem
until no one can hear the other.

Any sound that a sound might make has lost its mother.
My friend says she will blow a hole in the silence.
I tell her, look in the mirror
to get the feel of absence.

GLEANERS

FIRST SONG

Roll an egg away from you   the egg rolls in a circle
The bereaved one says   turn again my daughter
but you cleave to her   in poverty
you make your way   in her steadfastness
gathering to yourself   the sight of her face moving
over the stony hills   of her country
When her lips say *glean*   you bend to the field
pick three spikelets   one for your mother
one for your hunger   as for the other
turn it   everything is in it
an apronful of barleycorn

A PATIENT WORD

Placed a hank of her hair in his palm   folded the fingers around it

With a brush for a tongue and a red ink pot   painted a prayer on his belly

One by one   walks through the room to become invisible

The ink dries   on the brush that touched him last

Only a touch so light might   the quick and the dead

A patient word   the impatient flesh

There can't be nothing   says   *I will never wash it*   says

A bonfire flares   link arm in arm

The grizzled one   crawls over the ground

We must hold hard to this poverty

Laid her head on his chest   saw the black snake furled there

TEMPER AS A PORCUPINE

A man reached for an apple   the tree withdrew from his grasp
A red-faced interval   apple on a feral tree
An abandoned homestead   foundation stones in the midst of
field and gardens   revert to woods
rusted plowshare and coulter   bridle ring and a length of leather
A red-faced interval
A woman stands   unmoving before her window
watching it gorge itself   on windfall apples
turning them in its hands   compellingly like a human's
She feels them   stitching across her chest
How he wanted that apple   how many apples   how many stolen apples

His undoing

The sky is a vast wing   you can smell it
lie down over the length of you   become a horizon
First kissed of your father   but never his best beloved
Self-exile asleep in the desert   hip jut and shoulder the mountains' bones
dream-stone for a pillow   From a distance a stranger arrives
All night you lie wrestling with him   believing that effort becomes you
your flocks will multiply   earth groan under the weight of you
Esau will weep at the sight of you   With one finger you lift the stranger's palm
it balances   where a nail might enter
The stranger touches   the flesh that is always in shadow
No earthly power could have remained intact

NOTHING BUT HER VELVET SELF

A girl in a lantern slide   sheared from fire
traveled a century   with the gift of tears
What do you want dead one   *Remember Rose*
a flammable girl   newly arrived but already singing
Better to sleep than eat   *Remember Rose*
When contempt would not even   speak the word would silence
salt   pigment
the lock with the charred   shot bolt
how many rise to grief   *Remember Rose*
eager   striking out
wool trimmed with velvet   fitted to bones' white horses

WHEN I FLED IT FOLLOWED   WHEN I FROZE IT SLID FORWARD

Standing in the wind   makes a wilderness
for the tribe to wander   untethered by thought
quieted   by mountains' grief
the cold bracing   *whatever is to be seen of us*
tableau vivant   *figure us as you will*
black cloth   black oil and radiance
clustering   in the wind
a center   and a growing radius
now and again a leaf   scratches a surface
one tree is luminous   *we avert our eyes to a distant object*
a towering father   *we avert our eyes to the ground*

WHILE THEY SING THEY HAVE NO NAMES

They sang as they gleaned   not to waste any of the abundance
the common grape of the second harvest   potatoes souring in the sun
To the rhythm of snapping shears   their song rose clear water above
them bent at the pelvis all day   mosquitoes were biting
come night   old aches darkened the brew
mouth harp formed from the dark   they were centuries risen
the sum of the sum of labor   turned joy in the lamenting
As for the master   of sheep and white cattle
who keeps them   from his figs and apples
theirs by right   following the harvest
let his own weight topple him

GROUND TRUTHING

My thought returns
to that ribbon of black muscle   draped over a high limb
that long first day   I was a girl
its tongue was a water witch   I was bent on knowledge
of the flowering branch   the wind that sweeps the sea in its path
It has come to this
rod in the hand of   one who speaks with a scarred mouth
storm on the mountain   an arduous god
but this gift each morning
to every one his portion
that opens the matrix   the fruit thereof

THE CITY

I was one of the ones who crossed over.
They told me I was a chosen one.
I crossed into the city. What was I carrying on my shoulders?
The parts of the sentence were separated, I saw, by centuries.
I crossed carrying a sentence on my shoulders.

The city gates read City of Refuge.
They showed me a city with water for cleaning and drinking.
There was bread in the city to quiet hunger.
If you come without intention, they said, the city will open.
They said, here the avenger cannot enter.

I asked, but how have I come to this city.
They said, better to ask, where are the city's famed bookstalls.
Many a head has bent over a book and asked many a question.
Who am I to come to this city, I asked, and bowed my head.
Bread on the water, bread on the water, I asked.

HOLY

A man murmurs thumbing the beads in his circlet, the knots in his fringes

A man counts, thumbing the bills he's drawn from his pocket

What if he tells a story

A man carries a lunch pail to his store on a block that has been demolished

A son who remembers the aroma of wallpaper paste and paint

draws a halo around the site of memory

A man climbs the hill where a temple stood and under the temple a threshing floor

and under the threshing floor an altar

An angel appears to a man and slits him from sternum to pubis

What if a man says *Holy*

A man enters a tunnel rounding a vowel

What if a man dreams of an archer turning to face him

by the gate of a gold-domed city

The more he erases the brighter it shines

Betrayal

A seed pearl slides down the fallopian tube

90 years of waiting and now the slow roll into existence

Song and supplication

He wakes to the knife tip stroking his sternum

The other child exiled to the desert with no milk in the goatskin

Song and the spill of blood

He will be a wild man, his hand against every man and every man's against him

Or was it the other on the altar

And lifted his own child up

Song and

Cast the child down in the wilderness

And laid him on the pyre

The right hand smothering his dusky countenance

I have built seven altars and offered up seven sons

The left hand covering his face to save him from the fright

MAIMONIDES PRAYS

Praise be to God in gratitude for everything,
Esau still searching for his birthright,
lily leaves underwater opening and folding,
their languid rotation on their stems.
I open my wolf mouth. In the red-walled cave
of the patriarchs, webs strung from palate to tongue.
Praise be to God for their bones, finally naked,
their shrouds fallen in shreds. Praise for the one
who wraps them in nine layers of carpet.
I come with my blown glass lantern
from the street where we live like interlaced fingers.
Soldiers are skipping between rooftops,
slipping out windows; the birthright has flown off
like a songbird. Praise for the guttural caw
and its answering silence. When I sat down
at Abraham's table, I was given a loaf
and a small dish of olives. Now they ask,
What did you take with you, out of the City of Friendship?
A child who spits stones on the Sabbath.
The soldier who asks, How small, how tall,
what did you do? and the soldier who answers,
A small kid with his brother.

Meditation in Red

An old man is climbing steps incised into a hill
The man is bent under a sack of concrete
In this world some get to decide who can walk down the street

The street to the old man's house—razor wire and a checkpoint
Soldiers have welded the door of his house to the frame
He climbs to the roof on a ladder and down through a skylight

Imagine shaping a red eft in clay seven millennia ago
One soldier draws with a stick in the dust as if red efts were dragging their tails

EQUATIONS

My white cloth by candlelight is your white cloth by candlelight

I remember a meal the covenant once served me

My violin is your violin

The rain of the land in its season

Witness, set out

I rub the door post where the mezuzah held its prayer

A prayer is a tiny camera

My former rain is your latter rain

My latter rain is your former rain

My white breath with your white breath

So, our days may be multiplied

At childhood's gate, a snake

In the act of swallowing

A toad, legs first

Transfixed, we watch until

The one looks out of the other's mouth

Where we go the covenant follows

We begin to see it has intentions for us

INTENTIONS

I

In the beginning was the hand, and the hand was good

Celan says there's no difference between a handshake and a poem

The hand has a tendency to close around the palm,

flatbread and goat cheese, prayer beads extracted at the checkpoint

The mouth may say, *What am I doing here what am I doing here*

but the hand is curious, it learns with the fingertips

My hand remembers fingering the rosary, *frisson* of apostasy,

enchanted circuit of witless penance

At this moment, everywhere, the hand is touching the forbidden

The head shies off but five witnesses compel the hand to tell

2

In your quarters, the fatigues of a dead terrorist are speaking seeds birds carry off into the terebinth

Just now you were watching the sun set into undulating dunes fire surrounded

A monstrous and original danger, and the dunes and the glimmering sea

All the boys looked so sad, so very sad, so at a loss to understand what was wanted of them

Inside every house was a world, walls you could pass through

Life and the afterlife waved white rags

Everyone aimed for the legs or the chest to express intimate relationship

Windows and widows. Confirm kill

You fashion a counterpart, fatigues and an after-opening to deepen your translation

Words sound silently—*um/ima, bayt/bayit*

3

The time came to place themselves in harm's way

but just how were they to do this

In another country they might step out in front of a Caterpillar,

paint blue butterfly wings on their breasts and march on the capital

but in their country earwigs spiraled down the cochlea

eating the thought that grows on the walls of the labyrinth

and dreams wept *I'm so lost*

One dream cut to the chase, a jet-eyed dancer,

right arm stretched, index extended in the Sistine gesture,

created a dream arm and a meeting of fingertips

4

The lintel barely four feet high. Five paces across a dirt-floored entry

A single room six meters square, tipping in every direction from the center

She sits by a table adjusting her bunched wool stockings, their red softened by sun and repeated washing

Asks, *Are there any like me in America?*

I lean forward to hear her story. When remembrance grips her she arrives

Sometimes the interpreter seems transparent

As if her words entered my body directly, as if I simply understood

She feeds me soup, irrevocable hunger. Unearths her fear, imperishable seed

This is my purse. I put away my camera

Those of us who are leaving thread the path along the river

5

Of the man whose clothes hang off him standing in line at the checkpoint fingering his beads

Flipping them back and forward clackety click clackety chattering feline bird through dormer

Otherwise as if docile the canvas sandals shuffling every few head to toe dusty lids drawn clickety clickety

Insect legs rub stone on stone rolls easily no sign something (you too were attracted)

Never to speak God's 99 most beautiful names in rosarium spheres (you too heard them colonize the)

Of amber agate amethyst garnet jasper jade olive baked clay date pit pistachio

Birds' eyes on a merry-go- (you too were unnerved)

Of the mouth shut in a sun-baked (you in the witness corner)

Of water and cognates—*see hear read write ask*

The man steps forward watchful opaque (you hold out your hand for the beads slide off into your

6

What is it called, your country

Who peeled off whose indifferent skin

Behind the mountain, behind the year

Who and who make a multitude

It wanders off everywhere, like language

Plural, abdominal, breath-borne

Throw it away, throw it away

And the long walk begins again

Then you'll have it again

Light in moving toward

7

I am in my mother's room. It is I who live there now. I don't know how I got there

He hands me the book it flies open in my palm

The olive-skinned boy I am wont to argue with

There is this man who comes here every week. He gives me money and takes away the pages

This chiseled boy who carefully slices the pear

This preacher's son who will not pledge his loyalty

Yet I don't work for the money. For what then? I don't know

Who says if attacked he will not fight back

Today he says nothing

Here's my beginning. It must mean something or they wouldn't keep it. Here it is

8

Unprepared I happened into that room where the only recording of her voice was looping endlessly

A chthonic voice less voice than resonance. My body paced from object to object in its confines

Within the gates, among the remaindered graven images of those who had loved her lyrically

Can you describe ... ? the voice asked in the voice of the river

But what followed was not description

Rather the sum of the burdens carried to prison gates over the centuries and carried home again

Those years, those *vegetarian years,* rolled in in black marias

Interrupting the games of the beautiful

You have read the accounts: The trusted friend arrives. If there is tea, they drink. She recites the new poem. The friend repeats it. They watch it smoke and burn in the small, footed bowl she uses for such occasions

Not to make knowledge possible. To forbid escape

9

By the membrane of the shibboleth

We killed for a sprig of parsley

By the city we sacked

Among bells and glassware

Can you pronounce this: *bûter, brea en griene tsiis*

Auctioned to slavery

Chosen, circumcised

Under the terebinth where Sarah laughed—

We came to the gates of the city of refuge

Our hands hated them not, beforetime

10

Of the year to come I remember the blessing of green

Our hands, *yad/yad,* waded into the clay, *tiin/tiin,* and fashioned each other

We could hear each other cross through danger

We could see each other hang upon nothing

Terraced hills grew green with labor and the labor of the olive

We stood in the stone-lined pool before the likeness of each other

One sanctified history incised the other

The dark on the face of the deep enclosed us

Horizons opened around our first intentions

I remember your vineyard, *karm/karem*

PILLOW

An old couple walks hand in hand to their deaths, each carrying a pillow

Their backs are toward me. I stumble backwards out of the ruined temple

I stumble backwards into a ruined house. Feathers litter the floor, stir and settle

An archeology of familiars: books I scattered, tiles I splattered with blood

Whose deaths do we weep for? What is the cast of the skin of the beloved

Throw down the pillow; somebody's being smothered

The face of the beloved casts shadows on the walls

Someone is still on the bed. Under the pillow the face I go mouth to mouth with

Down through the double tomb, tongue to tongue

PARIS, 1947

Should you arrive in the evening

as everyone sleeps and the street is quiet

you would see one window lit and two men sitting at a table.

One of them is writing, the other bends over a book;

from time to time they speak to each other.

Should you arrive at that moment

you might think they were writing a novel—

Non! You will learn they are composing a letter,

one brother sliding his finger down dictionary columns,

the other shaping meticulous courtesies

with a fountain pen in an Old World cursive

to a family in America they imagine

tending their peonies and roses.

The women are gone; they have only each other.

They write one painstaking draft after another

until the letter is good enough for you.

In the capital of a small republic

Tonight I am walking backwards
If I were blind I would know better than to do this
I would use my toes to grip what I walk on
I would sweep my path with a thin white stick
I would dare the crossing but not court misfortune
But tonight it is true I am walking backwards
Bending my right knee so my heel disappears in my trousers
Bending my left knee so my heel disappears in my trousers
If I were sleepwalking I might wander in the aura of God's protection
But I refuse the illusion of God's protection
I put my cap on my head my head in my pocket
And set out over the cat's-head cobbles
Tonight I am walking backwards

ϰ

How steep the stairs are to this attic
The stone is crumbling my steps are faltering
I climb up extending my right heel backwards
I climb up extending my left heel backwards
I enter backwards so as not to see God
Here in a room where His ghosts are milling
Waiting their turn to sleep in the forest
But tonight as ever they can never leave here
And we keep walking backwards in circles
Passing each other without touching
Weighing each other without glancing
Maybe I'll take my head from my pocket
Maybe I'll use it for a flashlight

⨯

The dead poet is walking the street again
I am listening for him through my window
The orphans are sleeping the poet is singing
Under your white stars hold out your hand to me
I place my white hand on the railing
And work my way backwards down the broken staircase
Lowering my right foot cautiously
Lowering my left foot cautiously
All the streetlamps have been extinguished
The poet is a chimera a shimmering lion's face
With angel wings that drag on the cobbles
The stones are what knowledge I have to go on
Down the seven stinking streets of this plague

⋈

The street is crawling with cats bone-thin and skittish
But when I walk backwards they prowl forward
The poet has melted the alphabet for bullets
On every balcony he waits a weapon in his hand
In the courtyard children have chalked their names
In an alphabet that is not the poet's
They are playing a game that is oddly familiar
Jumping in and out of a loop of cord
Hooking it over their footsteps
I am walking backwards through a swarm of bees
Thinking honey is no amulet fury no solace
The poet is flying over the brick wall whispering
Hush   live it backwards   recall

FORAGE

With the killings, the woods became a forest

Forgive me, my dead, that I would enter

That I spend the coins on your eyelids

I read a diary of your erasure. The candle gutters

I close my eyes and continue reading

The atlas of the bone brigade

They gave me a thin jacket. Whose. Somebody else's. I don't know

You can't know a thing. Who knows. Don't be so sure

People are milling gathering gossip

Someone steps into the night in my body

Watches my breath rise to that gallows star

A finger smears black paste over an infant's lip

To hide someone

Is a woods or a forest deeper

To save yourself

Those who can sleep are sleeping

Would have died but for foraging

Mushrooms, blackberries, sorrel

Moss for bandages

Flattened depressions ringed by granite necklaces

We were the dreamers. We had to be soldiers

Out of respect I withhold the subject

Crawled out of the sewer through this manhole

Ran over sharp stones into the thornbushes

I would like to remain faithful to uncertain clarity

Dragging themselves through the duff

A GHETTO SONG FOR THE MALINAS

To everything its absence,
its malina apart in the dark.
A malina houses treasure.
Malina is an ark.

Malinas for furs and leather,
gold, flour, weapons
and purloined papers—
to each its malina.

Malinas for persons
who breathe without permission.
A malina nursery
now that birth is forbidden.

From the street, K reports
the gossip. At #9
three men hack up the attic
to burn it. At #5

students dine on
farina, butter
and biscuits. Nobody utters
a word of the malinas.

The ones who lived in this
malina before me in thin
jackets (*Whose? You never
know*) have moved in

to the forest (*Don't
be so sure. You can't
know a thing*). Their clothes
return to the malinas.

I lie down on a cloth
spread on the floor or sit
propped by the damp
north wall of my malina

turning the pages of K's
diary (*Who would record
such a story?*)
until my candle gutters.

Night long I lie
still, see small
dark eyes whirl
in the sky of my malina.

ANTIDOTES

A poet was briefly intimate with a machine gun.
A librarian stole documents. A glazier broke glass.
When a partisan beat a prisoner to death
accompanying his blows with *This is for my mamele,*
this is for my papele, this is for my Rokhele
his commander neither commended nor reproached him.
Because a soldier guarded a prisoner all night
he could not kill him in the morning.
A prisoner kept a diary so it might outlive him.
A poet's mother approached him at the barricade;
if he let her in, he would have to let in all the mothers.

א

I stood on the brink with thought.

Thought said *You misread the dream,*

the lean years are *the fat years.*

Thought always talked like this,

A scone or a stone in your pocket.

The fat year adjusted its weight

on the chair as it reached for the butter.

I felt so lean-fleshed

waiting for something to come up out of the river

and swallow something that came up out of the river.

WOODEN SYNAGOGUE

A patch of cornflower blue left on the crumbling plaster,
one wide brushstroke that escaped the theft of color.
Gold not yet scrubbed from an arch in the women's balcony.

A short length of the missing woodwork;
below, diagonals of broken lath.

We feel the walls for what our eyes don't tell us.
Here the ark was, flanked by tall twin posts.
If worshippers suddenly arose we would know the prayers.

Raw wood, dirt floor, a roof that lets in sun and water—
all this is common. Every day barns list.

A kindness, really.

Degenerate art

Trove

One day roan horses are running
The next day they turn blue in the closet

Under a scarlet roof, sheep graze in the bridal chamber
Lovers kiss under the many moons

Her painted blouse, her carmine mouth
The body strung together

He sees we see through to raw red
Under the plumage, under the linen hat

A dangerous man, half eaten
His head smokes like a chimney

One day lawn and peonies
The next, exile, like all the others

THE EXHIBIT OF DEGENERATE ART
(*DIE AUSSTELLUNG ENTARTETE KUNST*), 1937

They came in, said "Heil Hitler," went around the apartment, and took what they could.
This included pictures from a collection of beautiful pieces by Gustav Klimt and others. Then
somebody came up and dragged us down to the street to clean it.

The face was a chatterbox

The face was a dilettante

The face showed weakness of character

The face lacked manual dexterity

The face was a whore

The face was a saboteur

The face was a cretin

The face confused natural form

The face was a cheat

The face was a mockery

The face forsook the idea of beauty

The face could not sip through a straw

A *YOSEM, A MEYDL,* 1938

—after two paintings by Rachel Sutzkever

Now we are darklings, now we go darkly
clutching the cub that will eat out our bellies.
The street boy led to the studio with promise of bread
I transfused with ochre and ash—
layers to swaddle him, colors to rim him in
and cap his cap with a bleed of carmine.

Just so with the girl. We are disturbed. Everyone shows it.
The mother's dressed her in normalcy—
here are the braids, the ribbons
like twin poinsettias, the Easter flower.
But the eyes will be white, there is nothing for it.
I lay on paint until she is blinded.

THE ARTIST IN THE GHETTO

A near-invisible witness
stealing the souls of collaborators
The Commissar, The Unruly Fellow
The Jew Snatcher, The Jew Baiter
You-Beat-Them-You-Steal-From-Them-Do-Any-Possible-Evil
The Chief Who Terribly ...

sketching the writers to perpetuate them
the stage and the players
the last exhalation
of the great bear of a music teacher who exhorted the children
to wear their poor clothes proudly, like officers' uniforms—
head on a pillow, hair untamed.

OLD WORLD

—in conversation with Peretz Markish

The room I lived in. The faded plush sofa I sat on in the muted light

The small round table with its cloth of lace

On it, by the vase of zinnias, I set a half pear beaded with cinnamon

Run my thumb along the blade of a butter knife

Sounds cross through the thin green curtain: courtyard of cobblers, minyan of thieves

My three brothers, buttering their lips with the alphabet

The Shekhinah rests on the cobblestones. Every stone, a book. Every wall, a scroll

I rest my hand on my brothers' shoulders

One leaves for the East, one leaves for the West

The third drops down into the sewers

The third hoes gardens, costumed as a nun

The third breathes under a tin roof, tucked in a crawl space

Ink strokes on his sleeve: letters of a gypsy alphabet

Spelling a home

That I may never be driven from it

The town laid out for the radiant Sabbath

Here no one despises the woodman or the water carrier

Bearing the fate of the world on his shoulders

I gather bread crumbs. Rumors slip through the borders

Armies slide down the mountain to slaughter, tracing an S, a serpent's path

This is the room where I wrote my letters. I cannot write my name

Nor can the child find its mother

My brother has followed bees through the border

The Shekhinah's feet blister trailing the wagons

A thousand years of footprints

My brother stalks himself, lashes shame from the body

My beheaded thousand years

The wind, too slothful for his tenacity

No one can choose their eyes at night

It is I—in my continued vanishing

א

The book in my lap, we're all laid out in it

All. All. A mound. The whole town

A wagon load of mud-smeared, sleeping passengers

Leap, mound, he writes, over threshold, over ditches

Dance it all out before the flames consume us

Out, shirttails!

The lover's feet are flashing knives

Flee, we plead, before terror compels you to erase the uncertain

To the land where poets sing forever

Beautiful as Adam on the day of his creation

To the dance, he writes, *his neck across the tracks*

Dance for a flock of mountains

Enchant it, so it remembers

His tempest streaming pitch

The sun sets twice daily on his interrogation

Black thigh, blood token

The mirror's cracked, the lamb crawls on its knees to him

It finds his face

Drops its head on his breast to suckle

⨯

This clutch of hot pink zinnias traveled

From garden to market, market to spiraling stairs

In this room my brothers cast their lot

The moment, the determination

The clock's brass pendulum is gold in motion

They are searching for the light that softens

The green curtain, the word green as genesis

At night I listen for them

Slicing black bread with a merciful knife

Their thirty fingers drumming on the table

Turning the walls to text while history compels them

Slipping their coats off to cover the other

What shall I do with so much memory

Three silences, an empty line, a blot

I am the sign, they say

You call it death, they say, *but it has a different name*

LASHING THE BODY FROM THE BONES

Do you plead guilty to this—

No—

So why did you confess to—

I was not involved in—

Perhaps you pled guilty to acting in concert with—

You have seen to what extent I have been under the influence of—

Why did you give such testimony—

I shudder to think—I was searching myself for—

How is it you confirmed—and now are denying—

I became ashamed of—

So what you are saying is that—did things that were not—and became a nest of—

It takes only one plague bacillus—

An appropriate person for criminal—

It is difficult for me to accuse—he is a person who is—there are elements in his—

Could it be—

By nature he is a convinced—

Was—an active—

Yes—an active—at one time he occupied a little desk—

From your answers—to conclude that—these —and together with—

Everyone was speaking out against—

Are we to understand—the entire—was against you, and you were against—

On the first evening—I already understood that things were going to—

Where is the truth—

I speak with complete openness and honesty—

VERGE

I picked up time and tossed it to the river

A black duck flew from my mouth

I pilfered a photograph of women marching, the image blurred, on the bias

And so it was I entered the broken world

The black duck lifted itself from the water, exposing an ivory breast

How placidly it swam before taking off low and fast along the path of the meander

Point of appearance, point of vanishing. Slim vertical body of a leaping fish

White thighs. A long slide shuttles, breaking against the beat

White torsos

By the water, any event is like this: a boatman forever loops the surface when a dark mouth breeches to swallow

White faces. Above them black, below them black

White feet. A pair of shoes, a life. None of it ever far from dirt, the handprint on the thigh

Curtain of tatted string, the floorboards gone

Behind the curtain, earth bank

And then, how quiet the event. White footfall

The black duck glides in a distant meander for a moment that disappears

I HAD ME A COAT OF ANCIENT CLOTH

Because there was nothing left to ask I studied your faces

The weight had entered them

They had never been so   true to themselves

A finger pointed

Its white hand fluttered before them

Later we ate soup   it was light   spiced   creamy

A color we had never seen

⋈

Did you too want

to prostrate yourselves to the sorrow

to lie face down   in the center of the depression

ringed by cut granite

and have the grass grow through you

I had me a coat of ancient cloth

It takes the form of your need

⋈

A peasant listens to the steady footfall

of his horse   pulling a wagon load of carrots

past the field where the Yids are penned

Mother Mary he cannot help himself

and tosses a handful over the fence

                        then goes on his way

What are we   to make of him

א

Under the painting where forces are contending

In the archway into the Pale

Here by the white tablecloth

Beside the headstones   where earth is subsiding

Scumbled   propped by the last wall standing

When the coat frayed I made me a jacket

When the sleeves wore thin I made me a vest

⋈

Nelly is writing to Avrom is breathing coffin wood writing of roses

Avrom is writing to Peretz asleep in the snow

Rokhl is choosing   for the selection

Her two best brushes

When the vest wore thin I saved me a button

When I lost the button I made me a mouth

If I could   I would ask more silently

Lyric

—in conversation with Nelly Sachs and Paul Celan

All the while the boat is gliding on the sea

Listening to him I think, one can never be too tender

Now the birds chime in

A language played like a thumb harp. Like swallowing water

A language of pure sound curtaining scrolls

You flinched when I told you they poisoned the loaves

I'm sorry to have used my mouth so carelessly

⋈

So too, the wounded

So, too, the stones on their common ground

My dear Paul, such joy your handwriting brought me

My dear, my good Nelly, I thank you from the heart

So too, the language without a territory

Venez moineaux! Venez pigeons!

If one was a solitude, two was an enclave

⋊

At the crown of the letter, smoke curls into the sky

A powder of iron, pearl, arsenic, and centaury

Pick up a stone, any stone

A thin flour falls on our heads

Also, the blind weaver

Also, a mother's slipper

If words burn into the night

⋈

Conversation over a white tablecloth

Dear P, blessed by Bach and the Hassidim

Take this sycamore bark between your thumb and finger

hold it tight and think of something good

A small boy, his lips unpoisoned

So we mark our dark accomplishment

Drawn between us, a line like living hair

א

It is quiet here, Nelly, quiet

even when Eric comes riding through the room on horses and camels

sometimes on a mountain goat

Then I am obliged to carry him on goat-back through the landscape

which in view of the furniture

I mean the mountains

is no easy task

SOMETHING WE MIGHT GIVE

—in conversation with Abraham Sutzkever

After a day of illusion, a moment of truthfulness

Someone is resting on top of someone resting on top of someone

In our mouths we are harboring white eyes, violence, erasure

Yet the bee slips wholly into the flower

A girl is running, over the hill and down

To be nothing, so to become again

A scalded beauty is something we might give

ﬡ

An offering to the poet who seeds our courage

Words are running from shelter carrying snow-white eggs

A wildflower returns to bloom in the ghetto

The city that isn't that was is resting uneasy

We learn to remember

The tongue complicit: *cleansed, denuded*

Something nests in the chimney, its muteness sliced by a knife

Ϫ

What joy in a stone here, a skeleton stone

A satchel, a compact, two small gold earrings

Scavengers piece the question together

We empty and fill

What we wanted to say and were late: just an *oy*

The fingers are dead and the boat rows homeward

So I will come with my hundredth sense to my bliss

⋈

In robes, hands roped together—the lunatic march

Longer than legend, the short walk to ourselves

What have we come for with green willow branches

As if for another world, describing, describing

A goat for the yard and a hut on our backs

To sleep where the dead slept in the bed of our absence

No means to redeem ourselves

⊁

Tonight we will steal in and borrow books from the unliving

All day and evening they came here

And left with a green knife under their arms

All night they would sharpen their eyes on the eyes of another

For there remained amid the losses this one thing: language

Among slaughtered sounds a newborn silence

Genesis words to light the long slumber

Notes

Gleaners

Sections 1, 3, 7, and 8 revisit stories from the Old Testament.

We must hold hard to this poverty is from Ralph Waldo Emerson's essay "Experience."

Intentions

The borrowings in the poem are from Walter Benjamin's "The Task of the Translator," Ilya Kaminsky and G. C. Waldrep's anthology *Homage to Paul Celan* (Marick Press, 2012), Emanuel Levinas's *Beyond the Verse: Talmudic Readings and Lectures* (Continuum/Bloombury Academic Press, 2007), and Samuel Beckett's *Molloy* (Grove Press, 1994).

"um/ima, bayt/bayit" are the Arabic and Hebrew roots, respectively, for *mother* and *home.*

The italicized lines in section 6 are from Celan's *"Es ist allest anders"* ("Everything's different"), translated by Michael Hamburger.

In the capital of a small republic

"Under your white stars…," from Abraham Sutzkever's eponymous poem, was set to music and became the hymn of the Vilna (or Vilnius) ghetto.

Forage; A ghetto song for the malinas

Herman Kruk's diary, published as *The Last Days of the Jerusalem of Lithuania: Chronicles from the Vilna Ghetto and the Camps, 1939–1944* (Yale University Press, 2002), provided information and inspiration for these poems. Malinas were hiding places, sometimes quite elaborately excavated and constructed, used to conceal everything from food to people slated for selections.

Degenerate art

"They came in …" are the words of Ernest Granville, describing the day the Nazis looted his family home in Vienna.

Descriptive terms in "The Exhibit of Degenerate Art" are taken from Adolf Hitler's speech on the occasion of the exhibit and from slogans posted on the walls alongside the paintings.

A Yosem, A Meydl, 1938; The artist in the ghetto

Rachel Sutzkever was imprisoned in the Vilna ghetto along with her cousin, the Yiddish language poet Abraham Sutzkever, and several other members of the Yung Vilne group of artists. He describes her in a poem ("Legend") as carrying two paintbrushes to her execution in the Ponar forest.

Old World

Peretz Markish was a Yiddish-language poet widely acclaimed in the early years of the Soviet Union but later executed, along with twelve other prominent Jewish writers and intellectuals, on what became known as "The Night of the Murdered Poets." Lines in italics and other short passages derive from Joseph Leftwich's *An Anthology of Modern Yiddish Literature* (Walter De Gruyter, 1974). Phrases from the writings of Abraham Sutzkever and Chaim Grade enter the dialogue as well.

Lashing the body from the bones

The poem is a distillation of the transcript of Peretz Markish's testimony at his trial for crimes against the state in the last months of the Stalinist era, as published in Joshua Rubenstein and Vladimir P. Naumov's *Stalin's Secret Pogrom: The Postwar Inquisition of the Jewish Anti-Fascist Committee* (Yale University Press, 2005).

I had me a coat of ancient cloth

The last line of the poem is from Abraham Sutzkever's "The Great Silence," translated by Barbara and Benjamin Harshav.

Lyric

Lines in italics and other short passages derive from *Paul Celan, Nelly Sachs: Correspondence,* translated by Christopher Clark (Sheep Meadow Press, 1998).

Something we might give

Throughout the poem I have integrated phrases and lines from Barbara and Benjamin Harshav's translations of Sutzkever's poetry.

"For there remained…" is from Paul Celan's "Speech on the Occasion of Receiving the Literature Prize of the Free Hanseatic City of Bremen," translated by John Felstiner, from *Selected Poems and Prose of Paul Celan* (W. W. Norton, 2001).

ACKNOWLEDGMENTS

My gratitude to Martha Collins, without whom neither these poems nor this book would have found their way; to Denise Bergman, for her careful reading and questioning of the manuscript; to Jeffrey Levine and Cassandra Cleghorn, for believing in my work; to Jim Schley, for his meticulous editing; and to Al Bersbach, for his patience, support, and love.

Warm thanks to the editors of the following journals where these poems first appeared.

Barrow Street: "Meditation in red" and "Pillow"

Cerise Press: "In the capital of a small republic" and "Wooden synagogue"

Consequence: "Forage"

Crazyhorse: "Ground trothing," "When I fled it followed, when I froze it slid forward," and "While they sing they have no names" (from "Gleaners")

FIELD: "Equations" and "Paris, 1947"

Ibbetson Street: "Holy"

Kenyon Review: "A patient word" and "First song" (from "Gleaners")

Kenyon Review Online: "His undoing," "Nothing but her velvet self," and "Temper as a porcupine" (from "Gleaners")

The Laurel Review: "Verge"

The Massachusetts Review: "Lashing the body from the bones"

Nimrod: "Antidotes" (under the title "A head is a hard thing") and "Maimonides prays"

The Pinch: "Cautionaries" (under the title "8x8")

Pleiades: "The exhibit of degenerate art" and "Trove" (from "Degenerate art")

Rhino: "Old World"

The Seattle Review: "Intentions"

OTHER BOOKS FROM TUPELO PRESS

Fasting for Ramadan: Notes from a Spiritual Practice (memoir), Kazim Ali

Another English: Anglophone Poems from Around the World (anthology), edited by Catherine Barnett
and Tiphanie Yanique

Pulp Sonnets (poems, with drawings by Amin Mansouri), Tony Barnstone

gentlessness (poems), Dan Beachy-Quick

Brownwood (poems), Lawrence Bridges

Everything Broken Up Dances (poems), James Byrne

One Hundred Hungers (poems), Lauren Camp

New Cathay: Contemporary Chinese Poetry (anthology), edited by Ming Di

Calazaza's Delicious Dereliction (poems), Suzanne Dracius, translated by Nancy Naomi Carlson

Gossip and Metaphysics: Russian Modernist Poetry and Prose (anthology), edited by Katie Farris, Ilya
Kaminsky, and Valzhyna Mort

The Posthumous Affair (novel), James Friel

Entwined: Three Lyric Sequences (poems), Carol Frost

Poverty Creek Journal (lyric memoir), Thomas Gardner

The Good Dark (poems), Annie Guthrie

My Immaculate Assassin (novel), David Huddle

Halve (poems), Kristina Jipson

Dancing in Odessa (poems), Ilya Kaminsky

A God in the House: Poets Talk About Faith (interviews), edited by Ilya Kaminsky and Katherine Towler

Third Voice (poems), Ruth Ellen Kocher

Boat (poems), Christopher Merrill

Lucky Fish (poems), Aimee Nezhukumatathil

The Ladder (poems), Alan Michael Parker

Ex-Voto (poems), Adélia Prado, translated by Ellen Doré Watson

Why Don't We Say What We Mean? (essays), Lawrence Raab

Intimate: An American Family Photo Album (hybrid memoir), Paisley Rekdal

Thrill-Bent (novel), Jan Richman

Cream of Kohlrabi (stories), Floyd Skloot

Wintering (poems), Megan Snyder-Camp

The Perfect Life (essays), Peter Stitt

Swallowing the Sea (essays), Lee Upton

Butch Geography (poems), Stacey Waite

See our complete list at www.tupelopress.org